PUBLIC SPEAKING MADE EASY

A Primer for Debunking Public Speaking Fears,

Simplifying the Preparation Process

and

Developing Personal Presentation Techniques

Also Contains Guidelines for Speaker Safety and Mitigation of Assassination

Attempts and Violence from Hostile Audiences!!!!

By

ALFONSO K. FILLON MPA

AuthorHouse™
1663 Liberty Drive
Bloomington, IN 47403
www.authorhouse.com
Phone: 833-262-8899

Because of the dynamic nature of the Internet, any web addresses or links contained in this book may have changed since publication and may no longer be valid. The views expressed in this work are solely those of the author and do not necessarily reflect the views of the publisher, and the publisher hereby disclaims any responsibility for them.

Any people depicted in stock imagery provided by Getty Images are models, and such images are being used for illustrative purposes only. Certain stock imagery © Getty Images.

This book is printed on acid-free paper.

ISBN: 979-8-8230-3333-6 (sc)
979-8-8230-3332-9 (e)

Library of Congress Control Number: 2024918350

Print information available on the last page.

Published by AuthorHouse 09/30/2024

authorHOUSE

PUBLIC SPEAKING MADE EASY

Techniques for Overcoming Speaking Anxieties

and

Delivering Flawless Speeches and Presentations

DEDICATION

. . . .

This book is dedicated to the many people with whom I have crossed paths in my lifetime whose presence, patience, encouragement, sharing of skills and/or mentoring have led me to a point in life of putting this work together. From my high school typing teachers Ms Verna Page, Edison High and Mr. Foster, Stagg High, Stockton, California (circa 1964) and other teachers, family, many friends and associates (some posthumously), I take this opportunity to thank them for their time and encouragements are not forgotten. I hope this work to be a worthy credit and representation of their time and effort invested in me.

I extend a special note of thanks to all those in my personal life or various career endeavors who reached out or took a chance and gave me an opportunity to do, or become just a little more, event-though, they did not have to. That took a special kind of person; they were special; I was blessed.

This book is further dedicated to the readers who are taking the chance that this book has the capacity to change their lives for the better.

To Purchase this book:

Please go to Authorhouse Publishing, enter the authors name or book title, click and proceed to add to cart and purchase.

Thank You,

Al Fillon - Author

TABLE OF CONTENTS

WHY I WROTE THIS BOOK

The ability to speak confidently, calmly with poise and logic evades many people, especially those who have not had the opportunity to speak to different groups on more than one occasion. On those occasions when that opportunity does present itself, it may be a very important one. In a high school or college class the speaking engagement is one that will be evaluated by others and graded. On other occasions the speaking engagement may be one that presents itself on the spur of the moment but at a very visible, important forum or occasion. In either case, I have observed that the performer is likely to be anxious and unprepared. I experienced this situation myself in a college class when I and other classmates found ourselves required to make a speech as one of the class assignments. We all got through it but we all could have been better prepared. Over time, in personal life and career, I would find myself in such situations on many occasions. At the beginning, I was anxious, nervous and lacking skills.

As I began writing this book, I felt it important to take the time to ask myself how it happens that I, of all people, would be writing on this subject; a book about getting over the anxiety of public speaking; learning and personalizing public speaking techniques. Especially, since my first public speaking experiences were to large audiences, and information to be delivered in a classroom setting for training and certification of staff and my speaking sophistication left a lot to be desired. That setting and engagement involved 65 students a week for approximately 50 weeks. In all, over 3,000 professionals as my students. My presentation evaluation ratings from my students were more often than not, less than the proverbial and desirable rating of "10" or Excellent. I owe thanks to many of the students in these respective classes for their candid comments on how I might improve my verbal delivery and related instructional techniques. Though some of the comments were not pleasant for the ego to process, I came to realize that if I made a list of all of the recommendations and suggestions for improvement and applied them to my presentations, I might make one heck of a presenter and instructor. That's exactly what I did! Results didn't come over night.

As luck would have it, upon completion of this assignment, I found myself assigned to role as an Assistant Academy Administrator with the responsibility of processing 30 students a week through a large State Preservice Training Academy. Part of my responsibility was to utilize quality subject knowledge specialist instructors for respective subjects, evaluate instructor presentations and ensure quality training delivery.

There I was responsible for ensuring quality content, clarity of message delivery and student participant success. I find that this looking back is important for a number of personal reasons but in the context of this book, it caused me to realize that despite the responsibility I found myself in, I was in some ways not yet as prepared and qualified as I could have been to deliver such services with the level of speaking sophistication and organization as I might have ideally had. I was blessed to encounter a professional mentor, an experienced organizational Training Director and Communications Specialist who recognized my predicament and areas I could improve in for better results in public speaking. He took me under his wing and worked with me on presentation, skills and delivery as well as techniques for connecting with my audience. I have frequently considered this chance encounter and commensurate results to be blessing. I also learned to accept constructive criticism graciously and welcome any resultant benefits. I encourage you to do the same

Over time, my exposure to additional training venues were also helpful. I would urge you to access as many training venues as possible in whatever areas you desire to improve skills in. Observing good presenters and critiquing even mediocre ones gave me additional skills to mimic for personal improvement and success.

The proof of the pudding of "speaking success" for me came when after retirement from one career, I taught college classes and evaluations from my students were consistently outstanding. Additional data showed that students in classes I taught had higher regular attendance and higher grades compared to similar classes taught by other instructors. I took a lot of pride in this achievement and was subsequently promoted to Program Director and eventually a Division Director with duties for hiring instructors, curriculum development, student attendance and achievement. I believe the achievement of my students was directly related to my ability to clearly articulate understandable subject matter to them which made learning easier and resulted in students motivated for higher grades and successes.

I now look forward without reservation to making oral presentations or performing at meaningful events as Master of Ceremonies providing me the opportunity to practice techniques and further challenges to connect with an audience.

On more than a few occasions when speaking or facilitating an event, I found myself complimented by members of the audience saying that I was the (unfortunately from my view) the only speaker at the event whose presentation they could clearly understand. Sure, this stroked my ego psychologically but more than that, it motivates me to do even better each time I get an opportunity. The confidence you assimilate through your acquired speaking and presentation skills will bestow upon you many rewards.

Because you had the foresight to research the road to becoming a good speaker and reading this book, you will find yourself way ahead of those who have not and more likely than not, trust that you are likely throughout your life find yourself a willing and capable speaker in no time at all. I look forward with you to your inevitable successes as a presenter.

PREFACE

Normally a preface validates the writer's qualifications for writing about his or her subject. I believe, I have accomplished much of this in the preceding "Why I Wrote This Book" section. Much of my professional experiences came about as a college instructor, organizational training officer, Master of Ceremony or Event Facilitator. I believe further validation will unfold as you breeze through the material throughout the book.

I think many authors have asked themselves numerous times during the course of their writing of a book about the value of the subject they have decided to write about and questioned the value of such material for an audience. Upon embarking on this subject, I felt that the topic was a worthy one and that there would be a benefit for anyone who finds themselves in the position I found myself in many years ago, anxious about having to speak to large groups. In retrospect, I wish that at that time I would have had access to the information I now have, garnered from personal experience and the school of hard knocks; I simply did not. I also think back to the lost opportunities to make a better impression on my audiences and establish an impeccable image with all whom I encountered in small and large group encounters as a young person.

I also asked myself as I began writing if there was a need for a primer on this subject and would it be of value to anyone. I had some current doubt about just how valuable this work might be to its readers until several nights ago. At that time, I was attending a board meeting when the Director mentioned how valuable a recent forum on addressing the fears of public speaking attendees found their presentation to be and her amazement as to the number of people expressing their related fears. I was not at that meeting but this revelation reaffirmed to me, the importance and value of this work I had earlier embarked or but laid aside unsure of the need for it.

Over time, I have found that many people find themselves traumatized when they have to give a speech or presentation before an audience. However, I know that with the information I provide in this book, those fears and anxieties can be relatively easy to overcome.

I wrote this short, easy to read book to help the countless number of people from students to professionals do just that, overcome their fears and anxieties by knowing they are not alone in having those fears and or anxieties and providing a pathway for their success in putting such fears behind them. For those who do find themselves anxious and in the unfortunate dreaded position of having to make a public speech or presentation, this book will help to get you over such anxiety and enables you to make presentations like a professional. It also gives the reader personal self-confidence in their acquired knowledge and a checkoff list to reinforce that knowledge and confidence toward noteworthy performance.

Instances When You Find Yourself Speaking and Glad that You Read this Book

As I mention earlier, I was very recently reminded, through incidental professional contact, of just how important and useful the subject of this book is for members of the public. Here are some occasions or positions in life where one might find it useful:

Employment as a Teacher, Instructor, Company Executive or Training Officer

Attorney

Birthdays

Funerals

Retirements

Master of Ceremony

Professional Forum Address

Motivational Presentations to your colleagues, work section division or team

Sharing a personal story or one about someone else

Business Proposal

Personal Address or Presentation

Job Interviews

State of the State (situational briefing)

Stirring Emotion and Feeling – Stating a position, a narrative or proposition

Impromptu Entertainment of a group or audience

Humor Roast or Toast

At a Professional or Family Event

Incidentally, the toughest speaking engagement I was to experience was to officiate at my son's funeral service. I was able to pull it together and, applying all the techniques I ever learned over time, the facilitation and eulogy was as logical and coherent as one could be under the circumstances. The moral of this is that you never know when you will be called upon to give your best. When you are – You'll Be Ready.

FORWARD

. . . .

My Experience – The Pathway to Confident Public Speaking

As a student, I found myself in high school or various college classes having anxiety about standing up speaking or giving a simple book report. At other times in my young professional life I again found myself in that same anxious position on numerous occasions as well. As I look back to those times, I found I could understand and empathize with those who do experience dread and anxiety when called upon to speak to an audience. However, it doesn't have to be that way! I will make it easier for you to overcome this anxiety and give you the basic techniques and more that will lead you on to becoming an accomplished speaker. It may be hard for you to believe at this point, but in a very short time you will find yourself very competent and confident at public speaking and, most likely, you will even look forward to the challenge of giving more and more presentations with poise, ease and confidence.

We find that many speech makers are either professional presenters and do it for a living for one reason or another, or they are individuals who incidentally find themselves in a position to fill a role such as Master of Ceremonies at a company or community event. In many cases however, we find many of those who give speeches are often just plain ego-maniacs who actually enjoy having the floor in front of an audience but have no idea of proper protocols and mechanics when it comes to the actual elements of public speaking. In many cases, the speakers have a professional title due to the position they occupy in public life and are assumed to be capable, competent and eloquent – even interesting speakers. Thus, they are afforded the floor and the attention of the audience whom they bore and even often insult by virtue of speaker naiveite, crude comments and unbridled small talk which they exhibit presentation after presentation. On countless occasions, you will see many of these figures responding to questions posed to them by news reporters on the evening news, other facilitators or interviewers. Sadly, often, they do not do a very good job of it: you are left wondering what the question was they were responding to as their response is inaudible or lacks clarity.

I begin this book highlighting the necessary and important points that address overcoming lack of confidence and anxiety. I hoped to begin each section with a thesis statement that gets to the point to focus your time and help to produce positive results toward the reason you purchased this book. By doing so, I also hope to accomplish the objective of the book title, Public Speaking: Learning to Overcome Speaking Anxieties and Deliver a Flawless Speech.

Referring to the content in the Preface, I could not have predicted the opportunities that would unexpectedly present themselves to me for the use of polished speaking skills time after time. It can be more than likely, that after reading this book and working on your skills, you will find yourself in that position as well.

Author addressing Graduating Cadets as Director of
Criminal Justice Studies at Local Junior College

INTRODUCTION

How This Book is Arranged

First, I will share with you, variations of a time-tested options and a <u>Formula</u> from which I was taught at several organization training sessions and which I have used quite successfully. I have constructed most of my presentations on a semblance of this formula adjusting the elements as occasions permit and situations dictate. Though this formula is used by many speakers, teachers and organizations, I was unable to find one originating source of this technique to credit.

Secondly, I share with you some constructive elements and personal dynamics a person should incorporate as a part of their aura which based on my experience, I feel are necessary, even critical, for a presenter. This should also help you to incorporate the proper attitude, mindset and aura (environment) for yourself as a presenter to facilitate confident, effective communication with your audience.

Throughout the various sections of the book, I have included elements that are for more advanced speaker situations or can lead you to that advanced speaker level. Focus on the basics you need; add in the applicable advanced elements as they apply to the situation and your needs. You can relate to the speaking basics and always use them as your foundation and reference, then add in the more advanced and technical elements of presentation as you learn, as time permits, and/or the situations dictate.

Additionally, later in this book you will learn and incorporate reasons and your rationales for setting up the proper environment and tone of your room for presentation. When you have time to come back, reread the book or use it for further reference. You can also spend time delving into reasons, examples and specifics about the elements and concepts of effective public speaking. These elements will be frosting on the cake of being a good speaker. However, just as you do not need to know how or build a clock in order to tell the time, you do not need to master all of the fundamentals of public speaking at this point in order to give a good speech and deliver an effective presentation. I can assure you that will come to assimilate the fundamentals and that each element can be relatively acquired and incorporated into your aura as a speaker. Consider each of the aspects important - study them and apply them. You will be well advised to know what elements constitute a good speech or presentation but you don't need to sweat incorporating them all for each presentation.

Recently I was asked to speak at a formal birthday party with approximately 100 family, friends, business associates and dignitaries in attendance in honor of a person celebrating her 100th birthday. Using these techniques, I was able to inwardly reflect on the myriads of elements facilitating an effective presentation and, apply those that were necessary to achieve the best outcome for the occasion. The techniques shared herein worked perfectly for me. Their use will work for you too!

You will learn many things here that will lead you to becoming a model presenter and even basic elements to apply as a Master of Ceremonies. One thing that you must bring with you to the table is the basic elements of human survival; the ability to adapt and be flexible.

Introduction of the Parts of the Book

This book is divided into several parts. The First part provides the reader a basic and quick compilation of important information and elements that can be used to prepare for and deliver an organized and professional speech or presentation. It provides the basic elements that a presenter needs to be concerned about or address in developing the basic skills and enhancing his or her knowledge base and characteristics to be a confident and competent presenter/speaker.

The Second part of this book provides information that will help the reader to prepare the environment in which to deliver a professional speech or presentation and provide a mental checklist of mechanical elements that a presenter should address in setting up the environment to ensure that delivery of the presentation is enhanced to the utmost and detractors and distractions minimized.

Over all, paragraphs are structured so that the most important points of each topic come in the first part of each paragraph. Related and important information follow; most important at the beginning and "nice to know" information follows. In this way the reader can breeze through the book highlighting the critical elements and apply them as needed. However, the reader can come back to the section later to digest additional information in depth if he or she desires.

The Third Section of the book contains advanced level information that could be pertinent and useful for you or the person who may embrace the fundamentals of speech and speaking as Public Information Officers or professional speakers. While most people who move to this level generally have professional technical support for the occasions, it nonetheless behooves them or you to consider these elements in order to ensure "support services" do not drop the ball in supporting you.

PART I

ELEMENTS TO OVERCOME IN BECOMING A SUCCESSFUL SPEAKER

I n order to overcome the dread of making a speech, presentation or facilitating an event it is necessary to recognize that fear and anxiety related to making a presentation is not unique to you. Most all rational people experienced some level of each when they first started making speeches and presentations. You want to break those elements down and dissipate them from the point where they are inhibiting and debilitating, to where they are simply rational, comfortable concerns for delivering a message to your audience. Here are some of the elements that underline the fear of public speaking and methods to overcome them.

Lack of Self-Confidence

Self-confidence is the most important element and personal characteristic that a person must possess in order to make an adequate to flawless speech. We all want to think that we are "okay". We make our way through life doing the best we can and assume that is plenty adequate. Unfortunately, for many, when it comes to public speaking, many find themselves faced with the ugly truth. It is at that point that we experience anxiety, personal insecurity and self-doubt. Here we sell ourselves short letting self-doubt creep in and tell ourselves maybe what we have to say is not all that important. If you are there as a presenter, you are important and what you have to say is important also. Seize the moment, it is yours; it's your show! You are in command!

There are many different ways for a person to develop or increase self-confidence. Probably the most important thing is to recognize the level that these characteristics, low self-esteem, lack of confidence apply to you and then to take the necessary steps to address the respective issues. First think about your repetitive successes and accept the fact that you as good a person as any other. These days there are a number of self-help and motivational books and CD available which offer pretty quick, efficient and effective techniques for building self-confidence. One most effective is by Tony Robbins; Youtube, Freedommxx Instant Self-Confidence, 10/13/2017. With time, concentration and commitment and experience, you will find that you do feel confident in your ability to communicate. Once you attain that self-confidence you will find that you cannot only make a good speech or presentation but that you can do or accomplish almost anything.

Fear

One of the main culprits that contributes to the anxiety and reluctance of a person in making a speech is fear. Not the conventional fear or fright as in the "fight or flight" psychological syndrome due to perceived physical danger. The fear we have to analyze here is that fear which is derived from a personal feeling of inadequacy or feeling inadequate in the eyes of others. There are a lot of other elements that play into one's fearfulness of speaking in front of others but for most persons, the anxiety transmitted into fear is not because of real physical harm but psychological in nature.

In order to overcome this fear, one must recognize and accept that you will not be physically hurt by a "bad" presentation. Accept that regardless of the outcome of your speech, another day will come, and you will have survived the event. Realize that you have talked with many people over time and have come away with those people having been better off for talking and having made your acquaintance with you. If you can, take it to the next step and buy into and accept the premise that post presentation, you will be stronger having experienced fear and anxiety in the context of this situation and overcome it.

Personal Insecurities

In some cases, personal feelings of inadequacy are based on long standing criticism from others; parents, peers or from other children while growing. Perhaps at some earlier time in life you were criticized for underperforming in some way, shape or form, whether you did or not. You may feel that you do not look as nice as others; do not dress as well as others; are not economically equal to other speakers or members of the audience. In other cases, it may just be that for whatever reason, you feel vulnerable when subjected to the potential for criticism from others. The possibilities for why a person may feel inadequate as a speaker are countless. In this case, you feel that your audience may be critical of your performance. Learn to accept yourself and others will accept you and any presentation you make along with it.

Ingrain in your psyche that you ARE worth listening to, are adequate as a speaker and just go do it! It's really that easy but continue reading.

Inadequacy as a Person or Presenter (Feelings of)

Many people faced with the task of making a speech for whatever reason or occasion are anxious and fearful because secretly, they feel inadequate. Confronting the individual feelings of personal or presenter inadequacy directly is important. If you are able to carry on a conversation with one or more people, I see you as already being an adequate speaker.

It is clear to each of us that we are not the best at everything. A high-scoring basketball player generally has a blessing of certain traits and characteristics such as hand – eye coordinate ability, agility, and likely other senses that others most likely do not have. Other traits and abilities can be learned and developed. A Medal of Honor awarded combat veteran like Audie Murphy would not likely be selected as a psychological therapist of the year. But with time and training, he might be. We commonly accept that we have our specialties and areas where we may excel and other areas where we may generally be viewed by ourselves and others as average performers. Speakers can have some innate traits that could be beneficial. However, please note that you should not view yourself at any time as inadequate. I know that at this point, getting a reader who initially feels inadequate as a speaker, to put this feeling of speaking inadequacy behind him or her, is easier said than done; this might be the case for many people and would be speakers. But also note that you will not find the element of qualification or rating of "inadequacy" on any evaluation matrix form relating to your evaluation as a speaker. Simply put, I do not even know you! Yet, I can unequivocally say – You are NOT Inadequate as a speaker; look forward to the challenge. If you are speaking as a classroom assignment, other classmates will have to present on a topic as well. They will be in the same boat you are in. By virtue of the fact that you are, or will have, read this book, you have the upper hand in terms in knowing how to prepare and how to perform a cut above the rest! If you can carry on a conversation with friends, the grocery cashier, your doctor and others, you have the basics for becoming a good speaker.

One speech trainer repeated what he had heard from a teacher when he was expressing anxiety about speaking in public saying that he imagined the audience with no clothes on: I do not advocate this approach. This was to say however, that in essence, the audiences were just people like yourself and in that sameness, no better than you and having potential flaws as any other person or presenter would. .

DO NOT doubt yourself! Even just breezing through this book - you will have the basics and the fundamentals to perform well; you are more than adequate.

Author addresses members of a governmental employee

Elements of the Presentation

A Summary of a Presentation's Components and Inclusions

There are many elements to consider in the Presentation which is the body of your speech or address.

There are many types and tones of a presentation, from happy, to simple, to complex, toast or roast, or to a sad occasion such as the parting or loss of a co-worker or family member.

I always try to keep it in Four parts.

The first part is your Introduction. The Introduction of your subject including how you and the subject are involved; the correlation of you to your subject matter if any.

The second part is the body or "meat" of your presentation, speech or address. It's organization depends on how you intend to address the subject matter, bring relevancy of the subject matter's relevancy to the audience and stimulate the audience's interest in your subject matter. In the body you tell your story, correlate it with the subject in depth and in essence define the topic from A to Z so the intricacies and how they are involved in it are plain to the audience: your involvement with it also. Talk about the importance of the subject, it's history its correlation or redeeming quality to the audience.

The third part is that of tying your audience into the subject matter. You can thank them if they support the event or the subject matter in some way shape of form and call them to action in some way as the subject matter dictates.

The fourth and last part is the Close. Thank the organization and facilitator for having you as a speaker. Thank your audience for attending, being such a wonderful audience, showing their interest in the subject matter, continuing to support the cause (whatever you deem it to be) and being so gracious and benevolent to you for the time and attention they have given you. If applicable, I sometime weave into the closing here how the graciousness and warmth of this audience is so encouraging and makes what you do in the subject area so worthwhile.

If it is a high school or college class, thank the instructor for their investment in you, even fellow classmates for their support and indulgence. Be equally gracious when your audience may be presenters as well, especially if they precede you in the chronology of presentations to be made. Remember the idiom "what goes around comes around"; clap for your fellow students and presenters and they'll clap for you.

I'll say this many times throughout this book. You are important. What you have to say is important. Speak slowly, audibly and make eye contact.

A Note on Presentation Dynamics

I once observed a keynote speaker at an event I attended who was a Lieutenant Colonel of one of the military branches begin to address his audience. In observing him and his presentation, I concluded that as a U. S. Military Officer he commanded a captive audience when addressing military personnel. However, this was a civilian organization and an audience where he did not command attention by virtue of rank. He also left a lot to be desired when it came to public speaking and connecting with an audience. Respect, attention and listening courtesy is something a speaker must earn and foster. He could have benefitted by reading this book and following the TOM IPASTA instructional format I learned in the military that I explain later. When this audience became restless and questioning, he became rattled and repeatedly forgot to stay with his theme and subject matter. He tried to appease the audience by going where they took him to regain their interest instead of remaining focused on the subject matter. As he got sidetracked his loss of focus became evident. The audience even felt sympathy – yes sympathy, for him but the damage was done never to be undone. Noticeably, he lost the interest and connection with his audience. I bring up this incident as an example because I believe this person was missing as many of the simple and basic fundamentals of public speaking in his presentation that one could miss. This will not happen to you because by completion of your reading of this book you will know and have internalized just about all there is to know about the dynamics of public speaking.

I mention in another part of this book that one way to become a good speaker is to observe others who in fact, are good speakers. There are more than a few common people and public figures, that I have identified over time that are polished speakers. I will refer to a few of them in this book.

I am not pushing spiritual indoctrination but one person I consider an accomplished speaker you may observe regularly, mainly on Sundays on television at the time of this writing is Joel Osteen, a large congregation church pastor. After you get the basics together for making your own presentation, I recommend that you observe the presentation dynamics of one of Pastor Joel Osteen's television or other presentations (Youtube, Joel Osteen Ministries,https://moguldom.com). I talk about the potential benefits of becoming a good communicator and/or speaker. The referenced article attributes this person's speaker related annual income at $54 million. I think you can see that there are payoffs for being a good speaker and communicator.

Another person who I consider worthy of consideration and visual observation for his communications ability examples is Tony Robbins, Motivational Speaker and Presenter. (tonyRobbins.com, https://www.tonyrobbins.com). Different style, different venue. Yet, each of these and other persons you may observe have an engaging style of presentation, both effective and encouraging self-confidence and exhibiting speaking ability and style you can learn from and emulate. I consider that each has been instrumental via visual and electronic communications venues in development of my own skills. Find and develop your own mentors and style.

PART II

NUTS AND BOLTS FOR BECOMING A GOOD SPEAKER

Foundation for a Successful Presentation

The first element of a good presentation an ability to effectively communicate in the language you will be presenting in as well as the language spoken by your audience. Good sentence structure as well as an audible and clear voice is of the utmost importance. Knowledge and familiarity with your subject matter are the next important elements finally topped off by presentation of your material in a logical and free flowing manner that connects with your audience. Presenting your material in a clear and methodical manner is the key to a good delivery of the message to your audience.

Author presents at a State Seminar for Corrections Administrators

Picture from Left to Right: Richard Jones, Parole Administrator, Presenter Al fillon, Reg. IV Parole Administrator Bertrum Rice, Warden, Jim Donovan, Programs Admin, Dr. L. C. Vu, Chief Medical Officer

Two Format Options for a Presentation

There are a number of approaches to organizing one's speaking plan. For expediency's sake and for simplicity, I will set forth two basic speech preparation development plans here. The first option for developing a speaking plan is very simple. It is something we have been observing since we were young and likely in grammar school. Many will have observed the elements in action in Sunday School, church service or community forums. It is just that while observing it, we did not break down what we were hearing into sections or presentation elements. It is simply a dissected lesson plan.

Simply stated, all you as a speaker needs to do is to greet and Introduce yourself to the audience, highlight a Purpose for the presentation,, Introduce your Subject- matter, Present information relevant to the subject, Close the presentation and Thank the audience for their time and attention. Keep it Simple. Of course there are other elements that could come into play like answering questions or giving examples of Application - but this is keeping it simple!

Essentially, the Lesson Plan format gives you a road map; a place to start, your reason for the travel, points you'll visit along the way, where you'll end up; a Summary and a Close.

Presentation Option I – The Basic Lesson Plan Format

The simplest of the two formats I give to you that a presenter should be familiar with is pretty common and basic. This format is that of a basic Lesson Plan similar to those used in classrooms by teachers, instructors, trainers and forum presenters. The elements are outlined for the presenter as follows: Topic, Objective, Content, Summation or Closing. The Application, Testing and/or Performance component apply to a classroom setting but not in a basic speech, eulogy or routine presentation.

The following are the basic elements of a Lesson Plan format Presentation. Use these elements to build and deliver your presentation as they apply.

Materials Needed
Introduction
Subject
Objective
Content/Presentation
Closing/Summation
Test or Performance Demonstration

In preparation for the presentation the presenter considers the time frame that he/she has in which to deliver the presentation. The presenter can affix time frames to the various sections of the presentation so that he/she does not exceed the ultimate time given in which to make the presentation.

For simplicity sakes the Presenter considers what materials will be needed to successfully deliver his/her presentation, and gathers those items for readiness and use at the presentation.

To apply these elements to a presentation using the Lesson Plan Format the presenter begins with Introducing himself and the subject of his/her presentation to the audience. He/She then identifies for the audience what the Objective of the presentation is.

At the presenter's podium the presenter then delivers the organized Content of his/her information from A to Z noting the affixed time frames so that he /she is on track with providing the presentation within the time frames given. (Adherence to this technique is particularly useful if you find yourself in a role as Master of Ceremonies.)

Finally, the presenter comes to the Summation and Closing. The Summation is to ensure that you have clearly and completely shared and delivered the intended information relative to your subject matter.

While the Closing can be a part of the Summation, I address this separately because I believe it has some elements that are important. It should have an acknowledgement of the audience and a gracious Thank You to the audience. This is an opportunity to ensure that you leave your audience with a sincere and warm connection to you - for sure – and hopefully your subject matter as well.

In this Presenter Format, the presenter welcomes the audience, Introduces himself/ herself and the Subject matter, states the Objective, provides the information or Content, Sums up the germane points or highlights (Summation) and Closes the presentation.

Presentation Format Option II Tom-I-Pasta

As a Navy recruit still in high school, I had been given instructor training on putting together and presenting instruction in a military training setting using the system I present to you here. Some years later, I attended a U. S. Navy Non-Commissioned Officer Instructor Training Class that taught a person how to be an effective instructor. The techniques would have been an ideal foundation for developing a speech in civilian life as well. However, I didn't think about its value and the many potential applications it could be used in at the time.

Later in a civilian job, I found myself assigned as a Training Officer for the California Department of Corrections and received Instructor Certification Training again. This time I received similar training as a part of a Community College Life-Time Instructor Credentials Training Course given by University of California – Davis Instructor Winston Silva. This instructor had modified it a bit for our application purposes. I would use it as basis for instructing college, vocational, and law enforcement law classes in Laws of Arrest, Search and Seizure and other similar courses for a community college and the Department of Corrections. By following these headings laid out as follows, I found that I was able to develop confidence in myself and my presentation style. I knew that the elements were sound and methodical and that by following these fundamentals, the desired end result would be complete.

Note and Disclaimer – Tom Ipasta Instructional Format I am not the originator of this format. It was taught to me by U. S. Navy Instructors as a tool for an Instructor or Presenter and again by an Instructor from University of California – Davis in a class I was sent to for Instructors training to qualify for a Community College Teaching Credential early in my career. The originator deserves unequivocal kudos and credit as it has been a beneficial tool for a multitude of successful Instructors and Presenters, me included. I and others have been unable to find the originator for this instructional tool.

The Components of a TOM IPASTA Presentation Format

TOM IPASTA

As I explain in my disclaimer, I was not the originator of this method of Instruction or presentation. I was trained in it from at least two sources I have identified. Neither of these sources were able to identify an originating source.

The trainers who introduced me to this method of presentation to me began by introducing me and the class to the acronym "Tom Ipasta" which is the foundation of fundamental elements for development of a presentation.

The letters of the acronym stood for the following: T=Title or Topic, O= Objective, M=Materials, I=Introduction, P=-Presentation, A= Application, T=Test, A=Assignment. The experienced presenter will be able to relate to this application but I will fill in the application of "Tom Ipasta" for a simple speech or training session. In a simple speech you will not be using the latter T for Test, the A for Application, or the M for materials. In terms of the A for Assignment you may want to add that into your conclusion but in the context of tasking your audience with something to do such as volunteering time, contributing to a cause, community service, cause or organization, if it just happens to be appropriate.

However, the components apply almost universal. Simply pick the fundamentals as follows and as they apply to your presentation and develop them accordingly and to the extent needed.

For a basic speech or presentation, you will only need to use the following: Title/Topic, Introduction, Objective, Presentation. I outline and explain them in detail. The Tom Ipasta format is basic and adequate but incomplete. You must add a Summation and Closing. The summation repeats the highlights you want to reinforce in the minds of your audience; the closing in conjunction with it simply gives a personal reconnection with your audience, an expression of your appreciation for their time, attention and courtesy and the hope that the time has been well spent and you hope to meet again or some variation thereof.

Components of a Presentation for Tom I Pasta Format

Topic/Title

The "T" in Tom stands for "Title" of Presentation or "Topic" of your presentation. To build your presentation, start out with a Title for your presentation. The title should be one that is relevant to the interest of the group or occasion. Note that you will have to have selected an appropriate subject on which to speak.

Given the option, select a Title or Topic that evokes the interest of the broadest base of your audience. Hopefully, the venue you have been asked to speak at is one where you have the discretion to pick a Topic that you know something about; ideally a Topic you are an expert in.

If the topic you are directed to speak on is not one you know a lot about, study and research your Topic so you know it backward and forward. Do not procrastinate. Use your time prior to your presentation wisely. Fortunately, we now live in a world where, by simply using your cell phone, you will have a plethora, even an overabundance of information at hand with which to build a meaningful speech in short order. Again, do not procrastinate or delay identifying a subject you wish to speak on and do not procrastinate selecting a thesis statement on which you will build the meat of your presentation on. Caveat here – Stick to your points. Don't try to overly impress your audience by highlighting a lot of little-known information; know enough to feel competent. You should state your topic in such a way that just by seeing it or thinking about it – you are reminded of what you are speaking about and this will act as a subliminal and conscious reminder for you to stay focused on your topic. Note: you will be asked questions. If you do not know the answer, nicely admit that you don't – then, if not disruptive to the context of your presentation, ask the audience if there is anyone who can shed light on the question. If there is, share the answer with the audience. If no one in the audience can answer it, thank the member of the audience for the question, state you will have to follow up on it and then, without appearing unnerved, go on with your presentation.

Finally, the Topic should be one put into paragraph form for yourself and your presentation should direct itself in support of this thesis statement. If so, you will not stray far from the subject as your presentation unfolds.

Objective

The "O" in TOM stands for Objective. You can identify to your audience just what the Objective of your presentation is. Hopefully you identify one and are able to inform the audience of what your objective is. Feel free to state your objective and if appropriate in the context of your speech state the reason you are presenting on the selected Topic.

Remember: What is your Objective? If an Objective needs to be stated, articulate to the audience what it is; even that you consider it important and know that they will expect you to make the case in the course of the presentation.

At some point in my professional life after the Training position I highlighted in the Preface, I found myself on more than one occasion in the role of a Public Information Officer. Fortunate enough to attend a Public Information Officer training session put on for PIO's by an experienced television broadcaster and reporter in the art of public information fundamentals. One important element that the trainer stressed was to remember why you were there in front of the camera, what your objective was and to take the opportunity and obligation to consistently reinforce your point. Another instructor highlighted the importance of repetition and yet another instructional trainer emphasized telling your audience what you wanted them to hear or do, see that they got the point and if necessary, tell them again. This was especially necessary where the training to be given had to do with how to handle life or death situations. To really emphasize a point, have the student read, listen, write and demonstrate the point.

You should note that the ability to communicate clearly and effectively has been credited by many private enterprise executives as the reason for their rise to higher levels in the corporate organizational world. Remember to reinforce your objective whenever you get the opportunity.

So … Know your subject ….. make your points …. Stay focused, learn to avoid stuttering and unnerving hesitations and "uhhs", "and uh's" or "you know's". Make your points with a completed statement and simply stop there.... Period. Then begin your next statement talking about your subject confidently.

As basic as this admonishment is and because of its importance to you making a basic presentation, I will restate this again in another part of the book.

Materials Needed for the Presentation

The "M" in Tom stands for Materials.

This element is mainly for the benefit of the instructor. If there are materials needed for the students or the audience in support of applying the information you present as in an instructional session such as how to construct a craft item for instance, you should do the following. Establish a list of needed items, ensure items are available and in adequate supply, the how or by whom will any handouts be distributed assigned and the disposition of items readied. Have handouts ready for distribution.

A word of caution! Be cautious about distributing a variety of handouts before your presentation and before you are ready to introduce the specific material or item and guide your audience through it. I once observed children in an audience making airplanes out of handouts and finally sailing them from the second-floor lodge-type seating and sailing over the heads of the audience below distracting many from a visiting minister's presentation. In some cases, the audience themselves can get distracted by going through and discussing the material while you are trying to make important or serious points.

In this area you may and perhaps should include Materials that you as an instructor may need such as laser pointers, handouts, audio/video equipment and support.

The subject of materials will be expanded later in the book to include "hard" materials like electronic equipment, etc.

Introduction

The "I" in IPASTA stands for Introduction. You have already introduced yourself; this Introduction area relates to your Introduction of the Topic of your presentation. We have already discussed the Importance of Introducing your Topic. The Introduction is the beginning of your presentation. In the Introduction, two things can be accomplished. First you can fill in the blanks if you feel you did not receive an adequate introduction from the person who was to introduce you. Or you can embellish on the introduction or break the ice with the audience by commenting how the introduction was so great you felt someone other than you was being introduced as the keynote speaker.

Here, you will introduce your Topic, how it applies to your audience, a foundation of knowledge about it and a leaning toward what you will want the audience to take away with them.

Do not sell yourself short on knowledge or importance or begin by telling the audience you have a cold for example. Such comments leave the audience disappointed in you before you even get started. Do not start your presentation by apologizing for real or perceived inadequacies. Also do not say something like you do not know why you were chosen to speak; this tends to insult everyone. Worse yet. Never say that you don't know much about the subject. In doing so, you will lose the respect of your audience immediately.

If your presentation is in a high school or college class, thank the instructor for their investment in you and fellow classmates for their support and indulgence. Be equally gracious when they are the presenter especially if they precede you in the chronology of their presentation. Remember the idiom "what goes around comes around"; clap for your fellow students and they'll clap for you.

The Presentation

The "P" in TOM IPASTA Stands for "Presentation"

A Summary of a Presentations Components and Inclusions

There are many things to consider in the Presentation which is the body of your speech or address.

There are many types and tones of a presentation, from happy, to simple, to complex, toast or roast, or to a sad occasion such as the parting or loss of a co-worker or family member.

I always try to keep it in Four parts.

Part one is your introduction your subject matter; introducing the subject, how you and the subject are involved, the correlation of you to the subject matter.

Part two is the meat of your presentation, speech or address. It depends on how you intend to address the subject matter, bring relevancy of the subject matter to the audience and get the audience interested in the depth of your subject matter. Tell your story about your introduction and association with the subject. Talk about the importance of the subject, it's history its correlation or redeeming quality to the audience.

Part three is that of tying your audience into the subject matter. You can thank them if they support the event, the subject in some way shape of form and call them to action in some way as the subject matter dictates.

The fourth and last part is the Close. Thank the organization and facilitator for having you as a speaker. Thank your audience for attending, being such a wonderful audience, showing their interest in the subject matter, continuing to support the cause (whatever you deem it to be) and being so gracious and benevolent to you for the time and attention they have given you. If applicable, I sometime weave into the closing how the graciousness and warmth of this audience is so encouraging and makes what you do in the subject area so worthwhile.

If it is a high school or college class, thank the instructor for their investment in you and fellow classmates for their support and indulgence. Be equally gracious when they are the presenter especially if they precede you in the chronology of their presentation. Remember the idiom "what goes around comes around"; clap for your fellow students and they'll clap for you.

A Note on Presentation Dynamics

I once observed a keynote speaker begin to address his audience. In observing him and his presentation, I concluded that as a Reserve U. S. Military Officer he commanded a captive audience when addressing military personnel. However, this was a civilian organization and audience where he did not command automatic attention and he left a lot to be desired when it came to public speaking and connecting with an audience. Respect, attention and listening courtesy is something a speaker must earn and foster. When this audience became restless and questioning, he repeatedly forgot to stay with his theme and subject matter as he tried to go where the audience took him to regain their interest instead of remaining focused on the subject matter. As he got sidetracked his loss of confidence became evident and the audience even felt sympathy – yes sympathy, for him. Noticeably, he lost the interest and connection with his audience. I bring up this incident as an example because I believe this person was missing just about all of the simple and basic fundamentals of public speaking in his presentation that one could miss: an example I referred to earlier as a person of status absent speaking skills but invited as a guest speaker. This will not happen to you because by completion of your reading of this book you will know and have internalized just about all there is to know about the dynamics of public speaking.

I mention in another part of this book that one way to become a good speaker is to observe others who in fact, are good speakers. There are a few people, public figures, that I have identified over time that are polished speakers I will refer to in this book. One accomplished impromptu who you may observe regularly, mainly on Sundays but weekly television at the time of this writing is Joel Osteen. After you get the basics together for making your own presentation, I recommend that you observe the presentation dynamics of one of Pastor Joel Osteen's television or other presentations (YouTube, Joel Osteen Ministries,https://moguldom.com). I also talk about the benefits of becoming a good communicator and/or speaker. The referenced article attributes this person's speaker related annual income at $54 million.

Another person who I consider worthy of consideration and visual observation for his communications ability examples is Tony Robbins, Motivational Speaker and Presenter. (tonyRobbins.com, https://www.tonyrobbins.com). Each of these have different styles of presentation, both effective and encouraging self confidence and exhibiting speaking ability and style to emulate. I consider that each has been instrumental via visual and electronic communications venues in development of my own skills. Find and develop your own mentors and style.

Application

The "A" in TOM IPASTA stands for "Application"

This area is most often dedicated and pertinent when a presenter provides instructional information that the audience or student has been given in the course of the presentation and may be expected to perform a task, follow a process or construct something.

In some cases, you as the presenter will need to walk the student or audience methodically step by step through the process. Subsequently, in the Application stage, the audience will show that they have gotten the message and knows how to apply the skill or process.

If you happen to have an "Application" component in your presentation there are a few additional items to be concerned about for yourself and your audience. You will need to go through the steps of the process slowly with your audience. You should try out your verbal instruction on an individual as a test to see just how effective and clear your instructions actually are. Make the necessary modifications.

You will want to ensure there is ample space and that materials are available for the audience to use. If you are in this situation of using "Application" with a "hands on" component, you should insist that the audience be limited in number. You may even need to add a person as a "rover" to assist you with checking the adherence of your audience to steps in the instructional process.

It is important that you proceed slowly and wait for all of your audience to complete each respective step before moving to the next step.

Be patient with your audience (in this context, those you are instructing), sincere and very patient. 'Impatience here will cause you to lose your audience and result in negative feedback regarding your presentation.

As you thank them for the final time with a definite closure, there should be the beginning of applause. Slowly nod from one side of the audience to the other and thank them again finally turning to the facilitator and as he or she approaches you give one last glance or wave to your audience. If the facilitator is still applauding you, do not hasten to close the distance for a handshake until he or she finishes clapping. If the audience is still clapping be slow to pullout your chair and give a final nod. In this area things happen in seconds, so being aware of the dynamics of this process can make a big difference as to how you are viewed as an important speaker. The better you get on connecting with the audience, the more you will enjoy your moments in the sun and the more positive reinforcement you will achieve.

Test (If this Element is Relevant to the Presentation)

The "T" in IPASTA Stands for "T" Test

This element generally applies to an instructional setting where the audience member or student is expected to show just how much of the speaker's presentation he or she has comprehended, retained and is able to demonstrate.

While this is an opportunity for the presenter to see just how much of the information the student is able to demonstrate as retained, it is simultaneously, an opportunity for the presenter to measure his or her ability to effectively communicate information in an effective and meaningful manner. It is also the ultimate measurement of the instructor's articulation and organizational clarity including the ability to connect with his or her audience.

The "A" in IPASTA Stands for Assignment

Assignment (If this Element is Relevant to the Presentation)

This element of a presentation applies when the presenter generally has a special purpose and an expectation of the members of the audience to perform some kind of task often but not always using the information derived from the presentation.

In many cases it can become relevant as an appeal to the audience to join a cause or perform a task or respond to a call for action.

This element is usually beyond a conventional presentation but deserves to be covered to complete the IPASTA presentation format.

Demonstration

It is possible that accommodation of this component may be added into your presentation if your presentation is geared toward performance of tasks by members of your audience as instructed relative to following directions is that of "Demonstration". In this context you will want to ensure that you as a presenter has given enough verbal instruction and possibly written material in the form of a handout your audience can use for reference in demonstrating in some way that they are able to competently perform tasks to achieve the objective you wished them to.

Closure

(Closing follows next. This will be covered later please see that page)

USING PUBLIC SPEAKING SKILLS TO HONOR OTHERS

Presenter poses in Formal Lodge Attire before Officiating at
Celebration of Life Ceremony for friend and Lodge Member

"These unique and special occasions are the times that require that you give your best: every skill, poise and nuance is demanded. Organization, clarity, and enunciation; sincerity and audibility are an absolute must."

PART III

ADVANCE SPEECH MAKING

The Elements and Building Blocks of a Successful Presenter and Presentation

There are a number of things that contribute to being a successful presenter. Some of them are inherent in the presenter, others are external and environmental; While others are a matter of technical processes, environmental affects, software, hardware and direct and peripheral support. What follows is a compilation and breakdown of these components and essentially how they contribute positively to the speaker's presentation or may distract from it.

Self-Confidence

One of the most important characteristics a person needs to be successful in most any endeavor in life is self-confidence; a good ego can help also. If you already possess this combination of characteristics, you are a step ahead of others in making a presentation.

If you examine yourself and find that you feel you do not have the level of confidence you would like to have, work on it in any way you can. You can start on it in a number of simple ways; repetitive successes after success can be the beginning and maybe the only path you need. Simple positive self-talk and positive affirmations silently or verbally before your presentation can make a real difference for many; try it.

When it comes to the presentation, assure yourself that you have something to say. Know that what you have to talk about – you as the messenger and the subject - are important. Be confident in yourself! This is your moment in the sun! Shine!!!!! Look in the mirror and like what you see! In another section I share possible ways for you to build confidence. I do feel you should follow-up on it whether you feel you need it or it is just a review.

Selecting a Subject Matter or Focus Point

This basic tenet is very simple. If you are able, select a subject you know more than just a little about and have a lot of interest in.

Making Your Speech Distraction Free

Speech – Distractions and Distortions

I will write later that it is important to address your presentations to your audience as though you were simply having a conversion with one or more persons – just collectively.

That tone and context will get you by most of the time. Remember, this is a scenario where you in the role of a speaker, start out with a hundred points but lose points one by one as you progress through your presentation - if you don't put things together for your audience. When you start out, you may likely find that your presentations won't be perfect; that you haven't used as many tips you have learned on making a presentation as you would have liked or could have. Don't be too hard on yourself. As time goes on and you give more presentations, even short ones for any occasion, you will find that at the end of your presentation, you end up with more and more self-satisfaction in your skills.

Many speakers destroy the elegance of their presentation with annoying verbal baggage. Some distract from their potential status as a good speaker by using utterances like "a", "uh" again and again or stutter before they begin a sentence or after they end it.

I have also seen and heard speakers use the term "you know" – repeatedly. More recently, one of such speakers I observed was a well-known syndicated combination talk show host and news caster and interviewer on a nightly television network. I cringe when I hear speakers use that phrase – especially more than once. The point in this scenario is that my reaction and the reaction of others of the audience is, **"No**, I don't know" but I am waiting for you to tell me whatever it is you've assumed I know. A further point is that if the audience knew whatever it might be – they would not need you as the presenter. So, think about the words you are using and what they conjure up in the minds of the listeners. Use clear articulate sentences and explain your thesis clearly. Think about what you are saying to your audience at all times. You may have to slow your speech down. This will usually benefit the presentation by helping to reduce echo bouncing off the walls from your sound system and improve audience comprehension.

Over time, I have learned that slowed deliberate speech at presentations; taking time to think what I am doing and saying, and ensuring my thoughts are methodical, logical, and in context with my thesis statements guarantee enhancing most presentations.

Disconnection with the Audience

I will later share the importance and methodology of "Eye Contact". That is not what I want to discuss with the reader here. Here, I am talking about the "Looking at the Ceiling" tendency many first-time or novice presenters make. This is where the presenter looks over the head of the audience; spends too much time looking at the floor, looking down at the podium or his or her notes (even fumbles with them, stares up at the ceiling or just does not maintain a communication bridge and connection with the audience. This can be disconcerting to the audience and leave them feeling neglected, discounted or unimportant.

This is just the opposite of making eye contact. This "speaker delirium" concept can often occur when a presenter is inexperienced at making a presentation or more specifically, has a momentary loss of focus, memory, topic or chronology of events. The ultimate impact of one or more of these speaker transgressions is that it ultimately led to a mass conclusion that you lack preparation and professional presenter acumen or ability.

Mirroring/Memorization/Retention

Generally, mirroring is defined as one's personal behavior in which a person subconsciously imitates the gesture, speech pattern or attitude of another. (mirror: to reflect – the American Heritage Dictionary 2nd College Edition)

If you have decided upon a style of presentation you wish to pattern your presentation after, you can practice your presentation by looking in a mirror and reflecting that behavior.

There are at least three things you can do to build your confidence, improve speech memory and clarity.

The first thing you can do is draft an outline of your material with a priority of importance and practice your presentation until you are comfortable with it's content.

Second, write out your speech; make sure your sentences are complete and upon being complete, that your sentences are clear and each sentence is definitive independently. Keep the paragraphs short and complete.

Read your presentation to yourself in front of a mirror. Watch your facial expressions and body language. Imaging how a speaker you admire would present themselves using your speech, but in their tone, body language, aura and incorporate that imagery into your presentation.

Record your presentation on an audio recorder and listen to your presentation. Make improvements as you go along. You may note that even the President of the U. S. and other Very Important People use a Teleprompter and still stutter, stammer and mispronounce words and use confusing dialogue.

Repetition, writing, reading, speaking, hearing and seeing will help to anchor the content of your speech for a clear and focused presentation.

Important Points for the New Presenter

Not everyone who makes a presentation has an admirable memory which is sufficient to carry them through a focused fifteen-minute presentation. For the new presenter and those who are not able to remember their important points, the use of a 5" by 7" Card with points **Typed in Bold** should be sufficient reference for the. Most speakers have notes and as I stated earlier, some have the benefit of a Teleprompter. Along with the other items I mention in the Materials section later, be sure to have adequate prescription power eye ware and sufficient lighting.

Absent a Power Point setup, many presenters, amateurs and professionals alike now have Tablets and Laptops to use for reference and support. I feel those can be useful. Unfortunately, I have seen technical glitches arise that have all but almost ruin the most professional of presentations including one I was a participant in Seattle a few years ago unnerving some of the less experienced presenters. I did not sweat the difficulty as I was experienced and had hard copy backup if needed.

Even though the presentation is written and before you, do not rely on this process without first practicing your presentation at a podium and, if at all possible, in front of a mirror.

At one point in life, I was diagnosed with Traumatic Brain Injury as a victim of an accident. Subsequently, my short-term memory became "suspect" and I waivered in my confidence to memorize and deliver an organized presentation. It was during this period that I personally relied on the importance of clear visuals and meaningful notes. In some cases, Power Point supported presentations were a blessing.

If, as a new or experienced presenter, you have some doubt about your ability to retain and methodically present your material by memory for any reason, TYPE (write in script only if you have no choice) in large enough font to read. If you do this however, learn to look up at the audience at breaks (commas and periods) in your presentation, during introductory comments, and – during any editorial comments or clarifications you make. Keep them brief, to the point, and supportive of your material.

Sensitivity to your Audience

The written notes are especially important and often critical when you are acting as a Master of Ceremonies and tasked with introducing a number of dignitaries and other VIPs (Very Important People). Correct pronunciation of their names is very important especially at multicultural events.

Introducing correct company officials by their correct titles is critically important. Introducing them by the wrong title can be very embarrassing for the knowledgeable audience, the person being introduced and sooner or later, you, the presenter.

An example of the ramifications of making such a mistake can be observed visually and by audio video (Youtube udPert, Nov. 6, 2017, Jack Jones, Bob Hope Christmas Special Viet Nam 1965) by Jack Jones singing "Wives and Lovers" to an Army Nurse (Women's Nursing Corp) but referring to her as a WAC (Women's Army Corp) shocking thousands of knowledgeable spectators. The "oohs" and "ahs" were immediate and resounding.

Highlight and Prioritize your Points

Highlight and Prioritize points in your presentation and that are of interest to the audience, either historically, present or future. These can be highlighted in Yellow felt marker or other color to denote and remind you of their level of importance. As you become more importance these inflection points will come to you naturally.

PART IV

MAKING THE PRESENTATION

Making the Presentation

Greet Your Audience

Approach the Lectern with a warm natural smile looking from one side of the audience to the other. If this activity is to seem natural, the smile will have to be long enough to be noticed and genuine. The glancing movement from one side of the room to the other as you approach the podium should seem purposeful so that as you naturally look from one side of the room to the other and the smile not over-extended to raise question as to your sincerity or professional speaking confidence. While the audience may not overtly smile back, this gesture will likely relax enough of them and open at least a subliminal connection with you.

There are things you can do to enhance a connection to the audience. For example, acknowledging a member of the audience you know on the way to the podium with a friendly nod may help to settle the audience. Acknowledging others, even if with "friendlies" also can help to break the ice and rally subconscious if not overt support and positive nods as you make your presentation. If this sounds intimidating or complex, just smile and do your best. Be confident. It will all workout; you will surprise yourself!

Introduce Yourself Properly

It generally does no harm for you to thank the person introducing you and reintroduce yourself again. You may choose to clarify or expound on anything that was left out but under no circumstance contradict your introducer unless there is something that is glaringly mistaken and negatively material to your reputation overall. And then, correct the record, not the introducer. When you begin your introduction, do so by stating your name and title (if any), distinctly, slowly and loudly enough for the audience to clearly understand you. Look around the audience as if to say – Is there anyone here who does not know who I am, know why I am here or who is having trouble hearing me? Always look for feedback from your audience – nonverbal or overt. There is a reason for this – on this one, I'll let you come to appreciate the dynamics of this gesture on your own as you gain experience in public speaking and matriculate the feedback.

House Keeping\ Items

Introduce Your Subject Matter and/or Reason for Being There

Include in your introduction how you, being at this event and a speaker, is relative to the subject matter and the audience.

If it is a speech for a class – articulate directly and sincerely that this is an important event in your development and thank the class for being there to support and encourage you on this important milestone. Do not be intimidated by the fact that a teacher or instructor introduced you previously as a part of the class. For these few moments of your presentation- you are in charge; you will be setting the tone. This is your moment in the sun – ENJOY IT!!! Your audience and your instructor will appreciate it. If you do well – and – **You Will**, the instructor will feel validated by your success. If by any stretch of your imagination you feel that you did not, simply remind yourself that he or she is the instructor and that perhaps – the instructor did not do enough in your case, maybe that of others, to sufficiently prepare you for the task at hand.

Connect With Your Audience verbally and through body language and always try to Make Eye Contact with All of Your Audience

Throughout your presentation, look from one side of the audience to the other and the front of the room to the back.

Underline the Importance of Your Audience, Meeting or Subject Matter

Express a welcome to the audience and tell them how it is an important organization, goal, cause or event. Share with them that they and their presence are important and that they are important participants. Thank them for being there and – giving their support if appropriate.

Admonishment to Audience on Cell Phone Calls, Conversations

We have advanced from the interruption of Audio Pagers and the variations of paging noises to alert members of your audience who are on call. We are now at a point in time where most all members of the audience have cell phones with each phone having its own unique and sometimes disturbing way of attracting the attention of its owner. The alert signal going off at the wrong time is disturbing to all persons present at your presentation;

more likely than not, disturbing to you the presenter. Consequently, it behooves the presenter to say a few words about this potential interruption.

I have concluded over time that the best way to handle this is to directly highlight this possibility at the beginning of your presentation especially as a "NEWBY" to making presentations and possibly one who might be disturbed and slightly disoriented about where and just what you were talking about.

I was in the middle of a presentation to an Emergence Response Unit once when about nine of the 20 persons in the presentation had their pagers and phones ringing at the same time and sought exodus. Though disconcerting, because of my experience in the field found it humorous as did the group to whom I was presenting. If this happens during the course of your presentation you can softly apologize to your audience, commend those who must respond for their alertness to duty and go on with your presentation.

On a routine basis as a speaker, simply began your presentation by advising your audience that you and "we" as members of the audience acknowledge that maintaining contact with our loved ones and employer are important. Inform the audience that you are now taking a moment to allow the audience to modify their electronic device emergency recognition modes. Ask for permission to ask the members of the audience to place their devices on a "softer" contact mode for the sake of others who might have difficulty concentrating if they were to be briefly distracted by "chirps", songs or other contact modes.

I suggest you not ask them to "silence" their devices. I feel this could be perceived by the audience as an overreach of your speaker-audience relationship, construed as rude, even condescending and otherwise inconsiderate of your audience. In reality, should one not be thinking and actually silence their device, unforeseen harm to their loved ones or service population (as in the case of caretakers and first responders).

Convenience Items

For the average length speech, use of the restrooms or drinking fountains may not be utilized. However, just in case there is an urgent need, share with the audience where the facilities are located and the preferred protocol – if any - for their use.

Visual and Unauthorized Recording by Members of the Audience

We have arrived at a time when recording of conversations or general interactions are easy. You should be very sensitive to the environment you are making presentations in and the likelihood that some form of recording could or will occur.

The entity you are engaged to speak for will likely have a related protocol in place; familiarize yourself with it. I discourage recording under all circumstances! This is a personal quirk I have but I consider it to be for a good reason. We should always be professional in our attitude, language, tone and expressions. As time goes on, you may be called upon to do more and more presentations. You may not be able to predict the subject matter, potential hostility inherent in your audience or the environment you find yourself in or discomfort of audience members with the subject matter. More pointedly, your use of questionable terminology may be overlooked in general by the audience but may not be so casual and overlooked when your intention is questioned, the recording is presented in court, you are the defendant and/or misquoted in the press.'

A specific concern is that it is all too easy to isolate and misquote words or responses to questions posed to you or use your response out of context to your dismay.

Peripheral Distractions

You've heard of "Murphy's Law" A K A "Anything that can go wrong will go wrong". You can't humanly anticipate what might distract your audience or derail your presentation. But in my way of thinking, you should. That said, do everything you can to anticipate potential problems and alleviate them before they occur.

A distraction can be as inadvertent as outside sunlight shinning into the faces of your audience from behind you or, on the other end of the spectrum, a member of your audience actually going berserk due to something you say or was thought to have been said in your presentation. Again, look at one or more of the scenarios I've provided and anticipate any elements of the environment you could improve upon.

Proceed With Your Topic

Begin with the first thesis or topics introducing your subject supported by three one-liners you have selected; then proceed to the second; the third and perhaps more. Briefly tell the audience how they have contributed to achievement of the goal or success of the subject matter may be helpful organization.

Articulate and Modulate (Ref/definitions: Oxford Languages/Google), (Application – author, note below)

Tone

Tone is defined as your sound and mood as you project or as perceived by your audience.

Modulation

Modulation takes into consideration pitch of your voice, tempo of your speech and expressions relative to all of these as transmitted and projected in your voice. In most presentations and speeches these elements come into play naturally. Do your best to apply these. Very few speaker presentations have these elements come into play in their presentation. Listen to those who give speeches (often pastors, sometimes politicians). I believe President Bill Clinton at his peak, to have been gifted in this area. There are others; learn from their voice modulations; "feel" how their tone, modulation, projected aura affects your feeling, connection, empathy, and sentiment as you listen.

PART V

. . . .

LEAD THE AUDIENCE TO YOUR CLOSING

B egin your closing by pausing and visually canvassing the audience. This is the time, and your opportunity, to lead your audience to a closing. Clean up your loose ends; a chance to make eye contact, modulate your voice, create an aura and closing atmosphere of sentiment reiterate important points or make a last point and ensure connection with your audience.

Thank Your Audience for Giving you their Time and Attention

In closing, thank the organization, event facilitator and the audience for allowing you to join them and participate in this important event.

Nod to the audience and Accept Applause (Expect an Applause – you have earned it), turn to the facilitator and shake his/her hand and thank the facilitator as you leave the podium for your seat. If you make direct contact with the Audience – the applause will often last longer. No one will want to be caught by you being the first to quit applauding you – especially in smaller audiences. (Experiment with this concept for funs sake).

This is the mechanics of making a presentation. When you think about it, it is a pretty simple process.

If you are able to follow these simple steps I have outlined for you, you will be remembered as a competent and masterful presenter. You will even be marveled at by many in your audience. This comprises the learning fundamental elements of making a masterful speech in One Hour or Less.

Here the Author steps away from the Podium and Microphone and into the audience to more intimately connect with them and spontaneously address questions.

As you develop your confidence and skills, seek out all opportunities to practice applying these skills before all audiences. While little gets in the way of you starting with large groups, the author feels it is more beneficial for presenters and audiences alike to master speech techniques and the public speaking art by addressing small groups before moving to larger groups.

ADDENDUM – A Discourse on Public Speaking Dynamics

The Elements of Speech Making – Enhancers and Distractors

Many people making their first speech find themselves getting nervous and thus sweating and feeling anxious about the task. There really is no need for that. Yes, some people find it easier than others to speak in public. Perhaps that calmness and confidence is due to a proneness in some individuals to either be ego-maniacal and overly impressed with themselves or are simply too ignorant to realize they are lacking in the skills and elements of presentation or they are oblivious to the receptiveness or even discomfort of their audience. In some cases, they are in a position of relative authority and take the audience and/or their acceptance for granted. Thus, regardless of whether their presentation or organization of material makes sense, it simply doesn't matter at the moment; maybe never.

Often, they are unprepared with adequate material and information.

Often, they fail to keep it simple and to stick to the technique as given above.

I have seen these downfalls occur on numerous occasions and committed by a goodly number of people and from various backgrounds and professional levels.

You don't need to be one of these people. If you learn the technique above and get just 80 percent of it right at each presentation, you will not be disappointed in yourself, nor a disappointment to your audience.

It's said that "practice makes perfect". Practice can make perfect in most cases providing you are practicing correct technique. In this case you are practicing how to give a speech.

Practicing your presentation can make "Perfect" but don't focus on making a perfect presentation. Practicing to make a "perfect" speech is not necessary under most circumstances and focusing on doing so will only put you under unnecessary additional stress and anxiety. Unnecessary stress will only be a detriment to your effort and the overall outcome. If you have seen even the most highly sought after performers, comedians, Master of Ceremonies make mistakes, sometimes repeatedly.

Self-confidence

The topic of self-confidence can be an immense one. However, we are not talking about the kind of self-confidence that comes from external issues, like being a great athlete or wealthy business man, or simply having a lot of money. It simply means being self-confident in yourself as an individual in the context of where you find yourself at the present. Knowing that you have the skills to make a decent speech should be enough to bolster your self-esteem in any case.

Know that once you memorize the elements of a basic presentation, you will get better with each presentation. Eventually, you will more and more look forward to each opportunity to make a presentation. Your audience is really no different than you. Even if in a college speech or any other class and being assigned to present, others in the class are no different from you. Don't let their anxiety about making a verbal presentation rub off on you or influence you negatively. You have read this book and are so prepared to excel in speech making your verbal presentations.

Select a Topic You Know Something About

In college English classes I remember feeling very uncomfortable when one class assignment moved into the area of making a presentation on a subject of our choice. Just back from military service and a war zone, I felt anxious and unsure of myself in the context of a civilian college class with peers from the community; some okay with the war and others adamantly opposed to it or anyone involved in it.

During my time on active duty in the military, I had been given training at a Naval Non-Commissioned Officer Instructor Training Academy that would have been an ideal foundation for developing a speech in civilian life. The training began by introducing me to the acronym "TOM IPASTA". The letters of the acronym stood for the following: T=Title, O= Objective, M=Materials, I=Introduction, P=-Presentation, A= Application, T=Test, A=Assignment. The experienced presenter will be able to relate to this but I will fill in the correlation of "TOM IPASTA" with the simple speech. In a simple speech you will not be using the T for Test, the A for Application, the M for materials. In terms of the A for Assignment you may want to add that into you conclusion but in the context of tasking your audience with something to do such as volunteering time, contributing to the missionary fund, or to the cause or organization if it just happens to be appropriate. Some years later, I was to receive this training again as a part of a Community College Instructor Credentials Training Course by a University of California College – Davis Instructor Winston Silva who had modified it a bit for our application purposes. However, the fundamentals apply almost universally. Simply pick the fundamentals as they apply to your presentation and develop them accordingly and to the extent needed.

The point is speech making isn't rocket propulsion science. Speech making is basic and fundamental but with a larger audience. If you relax, and practice – you can do it nicely so leave the anxiety behind. It really is fundamentally, the polished ability to carry on a rational and logical conversation. The only difference is that the conversation is simply a conversant speaking effectively to a larger audience.

The important elements of communication are the ability to communicate clearly both verbally and in writing. However, I have seen good writers be unable to communicate verbally. I also have seen good speakers not be able to write intelligible sentences and/or paragraphs. We will only deal with verbal communication here.

Pick a subject you know a lot about to speak on and using and by following the elements in either Plan I or II, you will actually deliver a good presentation! It's about that simple!

Managing, Connecting and Controlling your Audience

As a presenter it is important to do all you can to develop a desirable rapport with your audience. This rapport will determine to a large extent, the success you achieve in delivering your topic and the how the audience evaluates you as a speaker and acceptance of you and your message.

Exuding quiet confidence is important to achieving this goal in addition to being well-prepared and knowledgeable of your topic. There are other things you can do however to set the stage for that success.

The first thing to consider is to using whatever influence you can exert to ensure a proper environment for your message to be delivered in. Temperature, lighting, location, position of yourself and any video hardware and equipment are a start.

One technique to use in managing your audience is to mingle with some of the audience prior to your presentation. You can do this by moving about the room to the various sections of seating: to the left, the center seating and to the right seating section. The purpose of this is to make contact with a member of the audience in each section. Get to know their name and a little generic information about each. Be mindful as to where they are setting and the people they are mixing with. In a sense you will be looking for these people to be your ally if the need presents itself. I find it a good technique whenever possible to mention a passing reference or acknowledgement of them in the course of your presentation. This technique "can" break the ice with your audience and limit any overt negativity that could arise during the course of your presentation. On the other hand, you should be careful to ensure that the people you acknowledge are of solid reputation and respected by your audience. You do not want this technique to backfire on you and find out later that overall, the people you acknowledge to support a point are though by a good portion of your audience to be viewed as radicals in thought or reputation and/or not well thought of by the group for one reason or another.

Another element of this connection is to use these people as a focal point and to use them as a reminder to make eye contact with members of your audience on the left, the center the right, the front and especially the rear of the audience. I would say that after you become accomplished as a speaker, you should divide your eye contact with your audience in another way: 60 percent toward and across the back of the audience, 40 percent of your eye contact across the front half of your audience.

Mechanics, Hardware, Software and Support Items

The next thing you must consider is the mechanical and audio-visual support and staging you have for your presentation. I learned early, not so much from my personal experience but from observance of other presenters is to ensure that whatever systems you have, particularly audio, that the audio system is flawless and that the volume of the audio is more than ample for the space. Unless you are a distinguished speaker addressing thousands, audio support for a smaller space is sufficient. In order to do this, test the system before your audience arrives. Practice using a few standard phrases about your subject matter so you know the system works properly and that you know how close or far you can distance yourself from the microphone or collar device and effectively deliver your message.

I have learned that whether you are singing a favorite tune at karaoke or speaking at an event, it is vitally important that you have ample volume. You should work with your audio support or technician to ensure that he/she knows what you want and expect. Using this support correctly will allow you to speak in a normal tone most of the time but give you the ability to modulate your voice and presentation for effect projecting elements of excitement, sincerity, emotion quietly and meaningfully. It will also enhance your ability to modulate, articulate and enunciate your words clearly and likewise effectively even in a lower voice while speaking or singing.

External Support (Non-Discretionary Call) Sign Language Interpreters

This is an area that even professional presenters can be affected by and many insensitive to. Consequently, they have had their presentations hijacked and negatively impacted. (Reference" **The Two Way,** Dec. 11, 2013, "Fake Sign Language Interpreter Marred Mandela Memorial …"; Mark Memmott. In reference to his presentation at a 95,000 seat

FNB Stadium in South Africa, carried world- wide with the referenced by many "fake interpreter" just feet from President Obama.

The inclusion of a Sign Language Communicator is a support element you may or may not have discretion to use. This is an external support element you may find imposed on you by virtue of the entity or organization which has engaged you to present. This support item has to do with the use of a *Sign Language Communicator/Interpreter*. If you find yourself in a position where one is mandated by the organization or entity you are present to or for, these suggestions are for you. My suggestion to you is that you insist that the "Signer" be situated in back of your line of peripheral vision; not too close or not too far.

The reason for ensuring they are not located forward of you is that the signer's actions will be distracting to you in a number of ways. If they are located too far away from you, members of your audience will be periodically distracted by them. Some members of the audience may even spend a portion of their time focusing more time on the "Signer" than you, the main presenter thus distracting you.

If they are located too close to you, your sixth sense of awareness may cause you to be distracted by sensing noise, movement, breathing normally or by exaggerated air intake and exhaling.

Most signers are professional enough not to interrupt your presentation for clarification but just in-case, prior to your presentation you may want to advise the signer on how you may want to address any misunderstandings.

Material and Support

I have seen countless numbers of potentially good presentations ruined or deprecated by the lack foresight and or oversight of necessary, and adequate support materials.

Simple enough should be the need for access to electrical power. This is usually accomplished by plugging your device into an electrical outlet. Follow this one item through with me on the things that can go wrong here and that thinking will set you on the right path to being in tune with the needs assessment aspect of giving a good presentation.

Electrical Power and Amplification

If you are going to give a Power Point presentation you are likely going to need direct access to electrical power to adequately power your computer and projection device. One of the elements that I have observed ruin an otherwise great presentation is inadequate access to electrical power sources. In such a situation, the speaker assumed that there would be access to power for his/her laptop and projection device for a Power Point presentation. In many cases, the electrical power source was not close enough or the facilitating organization did not have one on the premise. Other issues I have observed were that the extension cord was too short or that the electrical outlet was not long active for one reason or another. I would advise that the speaker anticipate and, have an extension cord of suitable power size, length and necessary connectors or adaptors.

Other speaker support deficiencies I observed, the speaker had the necessary items but did not have a table to set the equipment up on at the right proximity to support. In another case the wall to be projected onto was dark and of uneven surface with distorted the images so much as to not be intelligently visible thus adding to confusing and distractions from the audience.

Audio System and Acoustics

I have experienced numerous situations where even the most experienced presenters had a very interesting presentation but with unplanned and incidental distractions or a lack of enunciation, the speaker could not be heard or even understood. In many cases, it all started and the audience was lost because the speaker did not clearly and audibly articulate his or her name, title, if any, and clearly announce what he or she would even be speaking about. Just as bad, I have observed experienced speakers add in a subtle joke, light humor or attempt to clarify a point but due to poor volume, the audience did not get the joke or punch line, point of clarification and in fact became even more distracted and or confused.

A rule to remember: Be sure speak loud enough to be heard, articulate words clearly and make eye contact with the audience.

Preserving and Protecting your Speech Material (Power Point)

In some cases, the presenter or student will be required or choose to use Power Point as a medium with which to present or enhance a presentation. Attention to details applies here. In such cases, I personally use "Flash Drive" device to store and backup my presentations on. I have always made it a point to download my presentation to, and have at least two, Flash Drives containing the presentation with the subject clearly labeled in CAPITAL LETTERS in my possession. One of the Flash Drives remains in my possession; the other will be turned over to the technician providing support for your presentation. Even with this personal diligence I have had technicians encounter difficulties maintaining integrity of the Flash Drive.

Acoustics

Wherever you present, your speech and the comprehension of your words will be affected by the acoustical ramifications presented by the construction, design and materials used within the building. Slick surfaces, walls and ceilings will cause your voice to bounce off the walls causing your voice to bounce off them in many different directions and angles. Especially in smally rooms. The Element of "echo" is another element to factor in but we will address that separately.

Soft surfaces like acoustical ceilings, drapes, soft wood, carpets and such will absorb sounds and muffle audio and volume of your presentations. This will modify the initial volume of your voice and projection of your words. It can even affect the reception and interpretation of your words and speech.

Echo

There is a proverb related to auto speeding that says "Don't speed faster than your angels can fly". A similar rule related to speaking is "Don't Let your spoken words get ahead of your Echo".

There are many situations where good speakers with good speeches have the essence, if not the subject and words themselves misunderstood or not heard or comprehended at all.

In many cases this blurring of the message and the words of the speaker is increased when an electronic amplification (a microphone) system is in use. There are a number of linguistical ramifications involved but we will simply deal with the fundamentals. Some muffling of audio can also occur due to delayed signal transmissions between connected speakers, especially in larger auditoriums or outdoor arenas.

Many speakers, even experienced ones, often make mistakes when using a microphone. In some cases, they hold the microphone too close; in others they hold it too far away from their mouth or overlook the fact that they have one set up for use or forget to use it at all.

Some speakers are so inept or uncomfortable in the use of a microphone that they assume one in unnecessary. They will even announce to their audience that they have a strong voice and are easily heard. I noted that in each such cases I have observed, their presentation would have been enhanced with the use of the microphone as some members of the audience did have trouble hearing the presentation with clarity. I some cases, the speaker accommodated enhancing of the presentation by increase his voice volume which resulted in the speaker

"Hot Mike/Cold Mike" Cautions!!!!!

As an incidental or occasional presenter, it is unlikely you will find yourself in the position to be concerned about this issue. However, it is possible that eventually, because of the skills and confidence you will garner from reading this book and the elements and commensurate confidence you gain as a speaker and presenter, that you just may achieve professional speaker, Master of Ceremonies or newscaster/reporter status or acclaim. I have received training in this area, performed as an Organization and Public Agency Public Information Officer and done some related coaching in this area. If you find yourself in this situation, and I hope you do, seek the best professional training and coaching you can afford; it will pay off in the end. I am considering writing a book on this.

Video Systems and Equipment

Many presentations are tremendously enhanced by the use of video and more specifically the use of power point. It will take time and effort to learn how to apply the many elements that can be used but it will be useful to you. If you are going to do many presentations it is incumbent on you to learn how to use Power Point; it can be an extremely valuable tool. Your presentation can be downloaded on a flash drive and slipped in your pocket. I download onto two flash drives – just in case something unpredictable happens.

Make sure that before the audience arrives for your presentation, you go over the expectations with the technician and that your technician is able to bring up your presentation on the support hardware and projection device. The second device stays with me as an insurance policy against misplacement of my presentation information and medium. Further, ensure that there is synthesis of your formatting and presentation between one device and another.

DO NOT accept the word or assurance of the technician that there is no problem.

Remember "Murphy's Law", "anything that can go wrong will go wrong" – precisely at the most inopportune time. In some cases, the malfunction is technical and accidental. I have observed more than one case however where the technician or assistant, used the occasion to sabotage the speakers arrogance and momentary imminence with accidental if not intentional failure. Do Not put or allow yourself to be put in such a situation.

In one case I was asked for my flash drive by an intermediary so he could pass it on to the technician at a national convention's forum I was making a presentation at. I was subsequently as just prior to my presentation if the intermediary had my flash drive for the technician. This could have been an "Oh Sh—"moment for me. But due to my experience and preparedness, I was able to reply in the affirmative "most certainly" and to know that in any case, I had a backup. Don't ever allow yourself to potentially be at someone else's mercy where your personal ability and professional reputation

Managing your Audience

On occasion there will be side conversations that occur somewhere in your audience whether it is large or small. I find that the best way to manage such distractions is to use the volume you have on your audio system as a friend and to lower your speech voice while looking in the direction of the conversations or distractions. Where this becomes notice and you are looked at, just sincerely apologize and politely and calmly ask with a soft smile, "I'm sorry did you have a question about what I just said?"

While you personally may not be offended or distracted by the "side bar" of discussion going on, the overall message of that disruption to the audience is that what you are saying is not important and gives license to others to deviate from audience courtesy and dynamics. Further, it is a distraction to your audience and it is up to you to keep that in check – before – it gets out of hand and spreads to other sections of your audience. I reflect on the affect of this when I was sent to a large facility that had some dysfunctional organizational management issues going on and the top management was removed. I was conducting regular morning meeting briefings when one employee who was thought by some administrators to be a "dissident" toward the previous management would clear his/her throat, sometimes a little louder than may be necessary. It was at that point that I would stop the briefing and simply ask, "I'm sorry, did you have a question?" Needless to say, under the circumstances, no one would create unnecessary distractions and the message was clear that I was in tune with my audience and could misinterpret the smallest of potential distractions and expediently address minor distractions or address questions. A little autocratic perhaps, but under the circumstance it was important to control the venue – Not be misunderstood. be mistaken or "unclear" about addressing misunderstandings, message or disagreements from members of the team.

Setting a Tone

Setting an emotional and environmental tone can be useful and important, especially when your presentation is related to appreciation of an individual or situation or, the moment, or section of your presentation recognizes the loss (at a funeral or celebration of life) or misfortune of a member of the group or other happenstance.

I was a "PK" ("preachers kid") and active as a high-school Thespian. I was proud to serve in both venues as each gave me insight to the use of projecting many different faces. However, there is a need to practice your "affect" or impact on people and audiences as you present – it generally does not come naturally.

In such situations, I have used the higher audio volume technique to lower my volume, slower facial recognition and eye contact with the audience and controlled emotional projection toward the audience to simply address an appreciation for the mercy of a higher power for the blessing and/or opportunity for the group to be together today (tonight) and, the fact that we do not know who of us will or will not have the wonderful opportunity to be together (in this venue) again. In such situations, I often invite my audience to make the most of each encounter and opportunity to express our appreciation for each other.

Motivation

On occasion you could find that because of reputation, position or just situation you are expected to further enhance the spirit of determination or success of the group. This is an important opportunity if you intend to gain or maintain your reputation with peers, a new team or a team or organizational mission, objective or endeavor.

These days we have the benefit of "Google" search for motivational quips and phrases that are applicable to the situation. No need to reinvent the wheel here.

The biggest challenge is to work on application of the motivational passages or phrases and to apply them to the situation at hand or that you are in a position to address and correlate them to.

Do not forget to give credit to the author or source of the passages and or phrases and the context in which they were articulated and how people and/or events were enhanced related to them.

Apologies to Your Audience in Advance – Don't

I have seen many presenters in many different venues introduce themselves and then begin with an apology to their audience. The apologies made were for a variety of reasons. In most cases, I found that the mood of the audience was overall unforgiving especially if your apology has to do with being unprepared for one reason or another. Do your best to address the topic or issue at hand and most of the audience will never be aware of your unpreparedness even if you are. Again, do not begin your encounter with your audience by shooting yourself in the foot. It is unnecessary and usually insulting to an audience who expect you to know what you are talking about. I have even observed relative learned speakers say that they did not know why they were chosen to speak or they really didn't know much about the subject. Such bantering is an insult to your audience, especially the host who invited you not to mention a negative reflection and shallowness on your part. Work on learning to be creative and adaptive; always try to make things work. If you truly do not have information to share, simply convey that to your host discreetly or in private before the fact.

There is a subtle way to handle a "soft, sincere apologies" and that is to couch it in such a way that after the fact, after your presentation, you really appreciate the attention your audience has given you and compliment them as an audience for being gracious and bearing with you (usually after technical difficulties etc;) no fault of your own.

Presence and Decorum

Even-though you may have a podium in front of you, resist the temptation to use it as a crutch or a shield between you and the audience. If you must stay close to the podium lighting or microphone or your notes, try to pull back away from it from time to time turning to the left, center and right side of the room and audience. Whenever you can, walk naturally from left to right and toward your audience while moving your eye from side to side with natural poses. Avoid repetitious movements. On occasion, I will walk partially into the audience for intimacy but never walk behind your audience for any reason.

Personal Affect –

As a beginner, and even when you become more experienced, it is important that you use your face and facial features and expressions to support your verbal presentation. This is a part and method of managing your audience. Use smiles, frowns and expressions of doubt and elation whenever appropriate. You will usually find that appropriate smiles generated from the speaker toward the audience is reflected back to you through the warmth and pleasant facial expressions mirrored from your audience. This can do a lot to set you at ease and encourage a natural spontaneity in your presentation.

Attitude

This is not intended to put additional pressure on you but from the moment you enter the room members of your audience will be observing you. They will observe your every action and reaction, your body movements and behavior looking for traits they find favorable or unfavorable. They will look for friendliness, nervousness and how you react to minor annoyances – real or imagined. It is important for the amateur or even professional speaker to be sensitive to these audience idiosyncrasies and mitigate his or her projected aura in these and other areas accordingly. A pleasant attitude and expressions of courtesy to incidental encounters with your audiences and others during the course of your venue will usually pay positive dividends and assist in mitigating negative audience attitudes and uncomfortable challenges regarding your subject matter.

Humor

There are many comedians in many venues; most are well paid and highly sought after to entertain using humor. If you are reading this book, chances are, you are likely not one of them – yet. As a new speaker, stay away from humor. In an audience you will find many different opinions about an issue or situation you may think is funny and worthy of soliciting laughter. Use care and ultimate discretion in this area.

On an occasion or two I have paid to attend a comedy event by established or up and coming comedians. Even these forget the basics on engaging with an audience. One very well-known entertainer I saw on several occasions was an excellent singer and was great to listen to. However, on occasion during his performances he would do a timeout to tell a joke – or what was supposed to be a joke. To his chagrin or surprise, after telling his joke, most of the audience was still waiting for the punch line; few got the joke. Many of the audience would have laughed just to make the entertainer feel good as he was well liked. The entertainer himself laughed however and said, "Well, I guess I should go back to singing"; we all clapped. If you eventually decide to pull a joke off the internet and try it, practice it at home. Remember to keep your jokes clean, generic and discreet.

Incidentally, I recently attended a performance by Dolly Parton, singer, actress and performer in Laughlin, Nevada. She is one of the few that I found able to tell self-deprecating stories, wooing and drawing in the audience with short jokes and stories about herself and life. It was a wonderful evening and she had captured the hearts and attention of her audience like only few can do.

On another recent occasion, I paid to see an up-and-coming comedian. His scenarios were humorous. Though I have been exposed to profanity and vulgar jokes in the military, I was disappointed by his seemingly over reliance on profanity, crude stories and four-letter words to appeal to the audience. This audience laughed at what I considered crudely articulated scenarios and jokes using four letter cuss words – words that they would normally be highly indignant about if the common person were to shout them out such in the presence of their mother, sister and wife or others publicly.

Watch the context of your humor, avoid use of four-letter words, obscenities and profanity.

Stay away from ethnic jokes altogether!

Author opens Charity Fund Raising Event with Welcome Address and Invocation.
Seated to his right, Community Celebrity Contributor Tami MlCoch,
KGET Channel 17 Newscast Anchor; Event Guest Celebrity

Handling Questions

In your audiences there will be those who are compelled to ask questions.

It is better to hold off answering questions until you have delivered enough information to the audience to make your points or tell your story – especially as a new speaker or presenter. You can do this by simply having a member of the audience write down the questions or have the audience slip questions cards to this person. Simply acknowledge that you are having this done or that you will answer questions after your presentation. The reason for deferring question is that stopping to answer them will side track you, distract you and drag you away from your subject and the smooth flow of your presentation. You probably already know that many of the questions presenters get are way off base. Such questions make you wonder if the person asking the question is even at the right seminar.

Later referring back to the questions will help you to recognize where your delivery is breaking down and where your presentation may need to be enhanced or edited a bit.

Once you become a competent and experienced speaker you will be able to easily break away from your presentation or thesis statement and handle questions spontaneously.

Many people, instructors, organizational trainers, and professors are sometimes herd saying to their audience – There are no dumb questions! After presenting and training for a while, you will likely come to laugh at that statement. There are dumb questions and you as a presenter will get your share of them. When you get them, think them through, treat and answer them respectfully. Don't let indifference on your part or of a member of your audience alienate you from your message or your overall audience. I have found that in some cases, seemingly dumb questions are simply well-meaning members of your audience desiring to be recognized as interested in you, your presentation or your subject matter. In other individual situations. strange questions were simply expression of a desire to be included in your group and receive recognition from you or one or more of your audience.

Again, a seemingly dumb question from one or more individual members of your audience may tell you more about the dynamics of the audience, the cognizance of the individual asking the question(s). More importantly, it may possibly, signal your failure to adequately and clearly express information in your presentation. It could also indicate that you are not providing enough information.

This is an important point about questions! From time to time, it could happen that you get to the end of a dynamic presentation but no one is asking any questions either because there are none or the audience doesn't know enough about the subject to ask an intelligent question. One technique to address this is to put a couple of good questions on4 by 5 cards and ask a couple of colleagues to ask these questions if and when there is a lull.

Handling Questions

More likely than not, you will want to have a few questions from your audience. This will give you an opportunity to understand the effectiveness of your presentation, the knowledge level, social and academic level and dynamics at play in your audience. Especially if you have not had the opportunity to asses that prior to your "encounter" or beginning of your presentation. It will also give you an opportunity to establish connections for networking on this subject matter or another.

On occasion, you will sense that the person asking the question has some level of antagonism due to the subject matter of your presentation or some level of dislike for you personally as the presenter. The better way to handle questions and answer from this and other such persons is to initially express a thanks for the question and some level of validating the importance of the question and astuteness of the individual for asking it.

However, don't repetitively say "That's a good question!" Especially if the question is unrelated to the subject matter, inherently "dumb", not thought out or the answer was clearly covered in your presentation **and** the person asking the question was there when it was covered or just simply want to "challenge" something or you.

Over using the phrase "oh that's a good question" will annoy more alert members of the audience, make you seem phony and predicating, even condescending. In some cases, it can be a good time to admit and apologize to the audience for not having personally thought of addressing that vagueness or oversight. This approach and opportunity will do a lot to encourage more interest and "honest" questions as well as ingratiate you with your audience.

You must always, always, resist the temptation to put any member of the audience down, belittle them or ridicule them in any way. There is no way you will win in any way by doing this and you will alienate member of your audience forever. This is not the way you want to be remembered. Always manage your tone of voice – especially if a question has annoyed you.

Last but not least –

When asked questions, do not assume that the audience heard or understood the question that was asked or the context in which it was asked. To remedy any misunderstanding or broken lines of communication, repeat the question in the context of what you heard and what you are responding to. If you are possibly in doubt as to the "essence" of the question asked, repeat it to the person asking the question and verify with them that you understand the question and that finally you have answered it satisfactorily. A "thanks for your help" will go a long way to validating your respect for the questioner and sincerity for the audience.

When English is your Second Language

I was the product of a first-generation migrant to America and it's culture; my father's primary language was that of a foreign culture and language. I was therefore immersed in listening to language and speakers around me who spoke what has often be referred to as broken English or a lesser known form of Filipino "Pidgin English". Because of my observations and the recognition of difficulties that were encountered by those members of my family's culture, I felt it appropriate if not an obligation, to provide some first-hand recommendations to assist anyone reading this book who speaks a language other than English and finds themselves in the position of having to make a speech or presentation to a strictly English-speaking audience. I sincerely hope this is an encouragement and enhancement to your future successes in your making presentations to audiences of any ethnic or language constituency.

Seek out a language tutor for correct words and pronunciations. I have performed this functions for professors giving a commencement address along with coaching presentation tempo.

Enunciate and Articulate

There will be people in your audience of any age that have hearing challenges. For these people, the absence of clear and intelligible and of proper volume is disappointing, frustrating and almost a waste of time. The difficulty of understanding the speaker can be further compounded when the speaker has a case of what I call "the lazies" or being verbally lazy. This means that the speaker is not enunciating his/her words or articulating his/her speech.

The most important elements to remember and follow are as follows:

Speak audibly and slowly and to your audiences.

Speak clearly and effectively to your audience

Enunciate all the syllables of your words smoothly and clearly

Articulate your words clearly

If necessary, use a certified language interpreter. I using a translator for the hearing impaired, expressly position the interpreter slightly behind and away from you. Speak slowly enough for the interpreter to calmly transmit your message. (This will prevent you from being distracted. I have, and likely you have too, on occasion, seen Sign Language translators over exaggerating body movement, hand gestures and facial expressions to the point where the audience lost focus on the speaker's the main message and began grimacing at the signage translator exaggerated movements trying to keep up.

For definitions of the above references to enunciation and articulation definitions, please access mirriam - webster.com/words articulate and enunciate.

The best example to explain the above is that you cannot enunciate and speak clearly if you have morsels of an apple turnover in your mouth nor will your enunciation of your words and be clearly heard is if you have your head bowed looking downward at your presentation while at the podium and not at your audience. Refer to your notes if you must but - quickly thereafter, make eye contact with your audience around the room; give them a chance to read your lips. Equate this with lip-reading.

Non-Verbal Communication

Challenged or not, if you are maintaining the interest of your audience, your audiences will look at your face and correlate what they are hearing to your facial expression and what they *think* they are hearing. So, give your audience the opportunity to read your lips and face and interpret what your facial expression conveys. Equate this with lip-reading.

Be careful to not give conflicting facial communications such as smiling when you are trying to communicate anger or seeming uptight when you are trying to tell a humorous story.

As the Presenter - Look and observe the body language of the audience; take cues from facial expressions.

PART VI

BONUS TIPS

A Checklist for the Presenter, Employment Interviewees, Interview Panel Participant Interviewees – Aura and Demeanor, Post Script Critiques

The following checklist opens the door beyond the scope of just speech making to applying learned speaking skills to the readers daily personal and professional life as well. Once you develop the dynamics of good public speaking you might consider applying appropriate elements forum panels, job presentations and any other speaking situations like interviews for employment. This limited list of Tips may be useful to you as you progress.

TIPS

Be positive about yourself in all ways – Your subject, your ability to deliver a presentation.

Be satisfied in your preparation and readiness for this occasion.

Commit your speech points briefly and clearly printed on 5 X 7 Cards – Print time frames on the upper edge of the card.

Practicing for your presentation – Take a walk in the park - around the block – some place where you will not be interrupted.

Cover your speech point by point, including facial expressions, hand gestures, etc;

Use your cards to write out a written copy one last time – do not stop to change errors in spelling, etc.

Stick to Time Frames given.

Set out clothing you have carefully chosen for the occasion, shoes polished, pants and shirt pressed; sport coat or suit laid out as well and color coordinated to need. Have every item on your checklist down to two cuff links (if used), writing pin, handkerchief, comb, even hair spray, lapel pin if desired etc. View yourself in a three-angle mirror.

Hair cut or hair salon visited – presentation ready. If you have facial hair, it is preferable to have it neatly trimmed and combed.

Get to the presentation site – On Time. Have transportation ready and an alternate mode of transportation if your basic plan folds.

Look forward to your presentation and a positive outcome.

****

Lets's look forward to enjoying our successful presentations and our audiences together!

Author Presents and Entertains Audience at Hawaii Theme Afternoon Luncheon

After your presentation is over –

Smile about meeting your challenge and being successful

Critique your presentation.

Make notes of what you did well, maybe even how you surprised yourself; then what you could do better for next time.

A sample audience survey as to the environmental issues make help at first but truthfully you now know better than the audience what you should be doing or not – Just Do It!!

Look for more speaking opportunities – Take the one by one

Congratulations –
you are now on your way to being a confident and accomplished speaker!

Closing Summary

The ability to effectively communicate is very important both in a personal social sense and in a professional sense. Many heads of private corporations have credited their successes and rise to the Chief Executive Officer (CEO) in their respective organization to their ability to effectively communicate. In the public sector, State Senator Barack Obama's twenty-minute keynote address on the second night of the 2004 Democratic National Convention that propelled him to high visibility and acclaim. {Source: free WikipediA -The Free Encyclopedia -en.wikipedia.org/wiki/2004DNC et al).

Regardless of what your life aspirations may be, just getting through high school or college, or going on to a career or public service you will find yourself in a position where you will make speeches. The sky is the limit as to just how many times, how many places and how large the audiences are, you will find yourself speaking in front of a groups sooner or later. The sooner you become skilled, able and comfortable at public speaking, the sooner you will find yourself successful and that your life and the lives of those around you is likely to be. Just do your best.

There are other books, videos and online presentations on this subject; seek them out for additional exposure and improvement suggestions, techniques and information.

I wish you many successes.

Threats to Safety

Critical Environment Incidents, Threat assessment, Violence and Assassination Guidelines

On the afternoon of July 14 2024, Presidential Candidate Donald Trump was shot at and wounded while addressing a large crown in Butler Pennsylvania a town of approximately 13,500. Candidate Donald Trump was addressing the outdoor crowd in the same fashion he had hundreds of times before during his campaign for president 2015, as president 2016 and as a presidential candidate for the November 2024 election.

As a speaker, Master of Ceremony or presenter you open yourself up to the public and an audience that you are likely to know little about. The members of the audience may be very positive about the subject you are presenting on. On the other hand, there may be members of the audience who are not favorable to the subject you are presenting on.

There is a lot you can learned about the vulnerability of a speaker by just watching news clips on YouTube or other news media outlets. As a security expert and consultant, a thousand things that could be pointed out for concern as relates to high profile presenters Having been in command of environments as a Trained and active Critical Incident scenario Emergency Commander responsible for overall Emergency Operations, Threat Assessment Containment, Hostage Negotiation Teams, (SERT) Special Emergency Response Teams and Sniper Teams requesting greenlight shooting authorizations, I found the preparation, event coverage, coordination, response of Professional Law Enforcement, emergency evacuation readiness troublesome in this case yet classic for your development of a speaker protection needs assessment continuum.

This situation will be discussed by many, Monday morning quarterbacked by many and each element thoroughly scrutinized including proactive leadership and experience.

In the main chapters of my book, I have stated that the speaker should always assume that anything that can go wrong will probably go wrong; be ready to take action accordingly to mitigate negative impact situations and still bring about a positive outcome. Generally, you will not be subjected to lethal force or threats of violence. I did mention in one of the chapters that you should be ready to handle an aggressive disrupter. We have seen aggressive disrupters create both verbal and physical havoc.

The main element for the speaker here is to be proactive in the following ways:

Identify security supervisors, liaison with the supervisors, discuss potential risks, learn about harmful behavior that may have occurred on prior occasions.

Discuss and line out an expedient evacuation route and alternatives prompted by an unplanned event.

Be aware of or arrange for Alternate Quick Evacuation which may be a trap door under the bullet proof podium with a cleared route of egress to guarded waiting vehicles

If time permits, apologizing to the audience for a quick "short" break due to a technical difficulties or other façades.

Know your audience

Develop a sixth sense as to identifying contrarians, hostile audience member by body language, looks, attire and carried materials.

Use your voice, tone and aura to calm and mitigate hostile situations.

Wear Bullet Resistant clothing when warranted

Know first aid so you may help yourself and/or others

Using your phone as a life line, notify in advance and have one reliable person you will contact during an emergency, when you alert them advice of status, location, intent and of the threat.

Be knowledgeable as to when and how to strike a disabling blow especially if you are being kidnapped or being taken hostage.

Follow directions of reliable leaders and remain calm speaking as few accurate words as necessary.

Move quickly!!!

Always be concerned about potential threats from your audiences or an audience where ever you are.

A quick silent prayer never hurts.

When you return to the podium, be positive, reassuring and go on with your presentation without further discussion and drama.

Thank your responders! DO NOT CRITIQUE ANY PART OF THE SCENARIO.

About the Author

The author is an experienced and accomplished public speaker with many years of speaking in public forums. He has functioned as a Public Information Officer in a large organization, presented on numerous venues including Television, as a Master of Ceremony, Guest Presenter, College Instructor, Public Department Training Officer and long-term trainer in both public and private forums.

In professional life the author was an administrator in various large organizations, a top real estate listing agent, College Instructor, College Programs Manager, Top Level Public and Private Prison Administrator, Certified Expert Witness on Prison Administration and Security for Criminal Defense cases involving California's Death Penalty cases, Substance Abuse Intervention Programs, Director. Author is currently on the Board of Directors of a Retired Public Employees Association and the Stockton Filipino Center. He is a Past Worthy President of a National Fraternal Order Chapter. He has numerous past and current Certifications or Credentials. The authors has a Master of Public Administration, Bachelors and Associate of Arts. He has authored several other published books. His other interesting books can be seen on various book sales sites including Amazon and Barnes and Nobles. Each may be purchased online at "<u>Authorhouse.com Bookstore</u>".

Printed in the United States
by Baker & Taylor Publisher Services